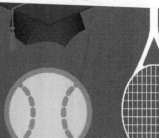

THE COLLEGE TENNIS RECRUITMENT GUIDE

EARN SCHOLARSHIPS
&
MAKING THE RIGHT CHOICE

CONTENTS

1

Luke and *Anonymous*

While there are a lot of educational consultants and companies that make a business out of selling education and recruiting advice and services, we are motivated by the fact that we both wish a book like this existed while *we* were going through the recruitment process. We had very different, but also very difficult recruiting processes. Both of us have had incredible experiences playing college tennis, and we want to make sure that opportunity is available for all who have the ability to play college tennis but need help with the first steps or with getting started. We thought it was about time that someone came out with a clear guide for how to navigate the system and lower the barriers of entry for players around the world.

Luke graduated from Princeton in 2018. He was born in Idaho but grew up and was recruited from San Jose, Costa Rica. For the first half of high-school, he attended "regular" school playing varsity soccer, basketball, and volleyball. In grade 11, Luke decided to specialize in tennis and spent the next two years playing ITF junior tournaments. He competed in the Junior Australian Open and the U.S. Open. During college, Luke was ranked as high as #13 in the NCAA in doubles. Luke is currently pursuing professional tennis.

Anonymous joined a top ten academic school in 2017. He has to keep his identity hidden due to NCAA regulations. As a student-athlete, it is forbidden to use your name and the name of the college to promote a product. *Anonymous* began to play tennis in London at age ten. From age 10 to 13 he played as much tennis as possible outside of school hours. At 13 he joined a school with an integrated tennis academy that allows students to play as much tennis as possible during a school day. From here his level kept increasing and began to make natural transition from regional, then nationals, and finally ITF tournaments. By his junior and senior year *Anonymous* had won a couple of ITF Junior titles and competed in Junior Wimbledon.

2

CHAPTER 1: IS COLLEGE TENNIS RIGHT FOR YOU?

This book is about how you can use your tennis to help gain a scholarship into a good university which is right for you, sign up for 4 amazing years of social, academic, and tennis training, and ultimately transform your school and career trajectories.

Media talks a lot about how colleges are an out-dated system, how too many people are going to school, and how everyone is getting into debt to go to college. However, that doesn't need to be your story. Athletes in particular are positioned to be able to take the most advantage of the college system. Being a high level athlete can make it much easier for a student to gain entry to a high-level university. Athletics can help bring down some of the costs associated with higher education (in more ways than just 'athletic scholarships'). Similarly, the benefits of being an athlete extend to your time on campus and beyond. Colleges often have extra resources for student athletes, not to mention the fact that four years of college athletics means four years of "free" training and coaching with teammates of a similar level. For many, college competition is the highlight of their athletic careers.

Today more than ever, it makes sense for tennis players to go to college. Athletics may be an education in itself, but athletics is also a great way to *get* a college education.

Is College Tennis Right for you?

For any serious tennis player, unless you are Denis Shapovalov, the answer is basically: Yes.

In the United States there are only about 1 or 2 players who decide that they will "go pro" every year. These players tend to be surrounded by a lot of attention and support, and there are often big financial incentives in the form of sponsorships deals which put pressure on them to go pro immediately after high school rather than going to college. The rest of American tennis players go to college.

In the rest of the world, thing may differ. Lots of foreign players may have the ability to play high level college tennis, but sadly lack the know-how or the help to make it happen. Instead, many of the players "go pro" and quickly spend all their money traveling to a few small pro tournaments. Before they know it, they have used up several years of their college eligibility, they are out of money, and they end up reducing their career opportunities.

3

College tennis does not mean the end of your improvement as a player, nor the end of your dream to play professional tennis. As the average age of top 100 players is increasing, more and more top players are selecting to go to college precisely because it allows them to improve their game, train and compete with players of similar level, as well as get an education and a "back up" plan.

There are now huge advantages in selecting to spend 4 years developing and learning in college. These include: a combination of high level tennis and academics: dedicated programs for certains schools to help athletes find jobs; specialized tutors for teams; networking opportunities (student athlete graduates are often favorites for top jobs because recruiters know the attributes such as time management, teamwork, discipline and resilience which they will have developed in order to thrive as a student athlete.

Am I good enough to play college tennis?

If you are reading this and wondering, "am I good enough to play college tennis?"" the answers is almost certainly: yes! One of the best parts about college tennis, is that there is a good fit for almost every serious and competitive player. This doesn't mean that you'll be able to go to a huge Division 1 school on full scholarship or an Ivy-League, but it does mean that playing college athletics, and using your sport to further and even fund your passion as well as your education, is a completely reasonable possibility. Many players just don't go this route because they don't know how to begin.

The levels of college tennis

There are three different associations into which college tennis programs organize themselves.
The NCAA, the NAIA, and the NJCAA.

The NCAA, is the most prestigious of the three associations. The majority of the top players end up at an NCAA division 1 school.

While the NCAA is strict about eligibility and amateurism, some good players end up in the NAIA and the NJCAA because these associations tend to have more lenient rules around eligibility.

The NCAA is in itself divided into 3 "divisions," based on level and rules about scholarships.

There are over 950 NCAA programs for men nationwide, while women can choose from around 1,100:

4

- For men, there are about 263 Division I, 161 Division II, and 314 Division III tennis scholarship programs.
- For the women, there are 320 Division I, 212 Division II, and 361 Division III scholarship programs. The NCAA allows for about 8 scholarships for each Division I and 6 for each Division II.

The NCAA allows a fully funded Division I and Division II men's tennis programs to give out 4.5 scholarships every year. For women's teams, each program can give out 8 full scholarships per year. This difference is due to the fact that many schools have American football programs where more than 80 scholarships are given out each year. Due to U.S laws, each institution has to provide the same amount of scholarships to men and women. Due to the fact that there is no equivalent sport for American football on the women's side, other men's sports end up with less scholarships.

- NCAA division III teams do not offer athletic scholarships. However, these schools invariably have some academic scholarships. Being an athlete and working with the coach can help you qualify for those, though they are not "athletic" scholarships.

National Association of Intercollegiate Athletics (NAIA)

Even though the NAIA offers fewer scholarships than the more well-known NCAA, there are less strict requirements for eligibility with the NAIA. Therefore, in some cases it is easier to join a team and maintain your membership, and therefore scholarship. For instance, students must meet only two out of the three following prerequisites: graduation from the top half of their high school class, at least an 18 on the ACT test or a 860 on the SAT, and a 2.0 GPA. The NAIAoffers 92 men's tennis programs, and 110 for women's tennis.

National Junior College Athletic Association (NJCAA)

Any student interested in seeing how far tennis can take them at the two-year community college level is invited to pursue a NJCAAscholarship. The organization provides funds for both men's and women's tennis athletes through one of its 141 women's programs and 120 men's programs in the US. The biggest draw for NJCAA or "Junior Colleges" is the low costs, and the ease of eligibility. Even if you are not on a large scholarships, the total costs of attending a junior college are often significantly lower than other schools. The drawbacks are the relatively low academic prestige, as well as a lack of depth of good players.

5

A lot of players who get behind on the recruiting process, can at least make progress towards attending the school they want by starting at a junior college. They can spend the year at the junior college, and use their good results and contacts to then transfer to an NCAA school.

Athletes who have played professionally also will find the NJCAA much more welcoming than the NCAA when it comes to granting eligibility.

The sheer quantity of programs and scholarships available here may seem vast and almost too easy, but be aware that while the NCAA awards are certainly generous, you will need to be an outstanding tennis player in order to receive one. There are a large number of significant funds available if you go this route, and the best of the best are eligible to get up to their entire tuition paid for in this manner. GPA, test scores, personal statements, and class ranking may all be considered in the awarding of these scholarships. You will want to make sure you are at the top of your game in all respects before expecting one of these highly-sought after scholarships.

Useful links to get started:

https://international.ncaa.com/
https://www.ncaa.com/
http://www.njcaa.org/sports_news.cfm?
sid=44&divid=1&gender=w&slid=25_____http://www.naia.org/

6

CHAPTER 2: BEGINNING THE SEARCH

With so many universities to choose from it can seem overwhelming to try and narrow down what you are looking for, get in touch with the relevant colleges and coaches, and ultimately find a good fit for you. By identifying your priorities, you can narrow the schools you are going to look at.

There are 6 primary factors to consider that can help narrow down the right school for you:
1-Academics
2-Size
3-Costs
4-Level of the team
5-Coaching dynamic
6-Location
*7-Religious Affiliation)

1-Academics

If you have an excellent academic track-record, and attending an academically rigorous or prestigious institution is important to you, then that is an easy way to narrow down your search.

Some schools will *only* be interested in if you have a solid academic track record Even if you are top 50 in the world, if your academics are not good enough, some school are just not going to be be interested. Other athletes want to makes sure that the academic portion of college doesn't affect their athletic improvement. It's Important to know the type of university you want to attend.

Rather than being overwhelmed by thousands of different possibilities, you can start by narrowing the search to a certain calibre of academic institution. The first great resource for narrowing schools down academically is the **U.S. News Best Colleges** website. U.S. News allows you to search by name of the school, but also by location, and then gives you a break down of size, acceptance rigor, average out of pocket costs, avg SAT/ACT scores, etc.

2-Size

Another factor for a lot of students is size. Before choosing Princeton, Luke closely considered going to Westmont College in Santa Barbara, California. Luke had always wanted to go to school in California, I had a good scholarships to go there for free, and it was religiously affiliated which he liked. But the population was less than

7

2,000 undergraduates. A lot of high-schools in United States are that big. While he wasn't super invested in going to a big "State" school which had a successful football or basketball program, Luke decided that the small size was enough of a factor to seriously sway his decision."

A lot of students are drawn to bigger, perhaps more well-known schools. There's some undeniable draws to having a big-time football or basketball program, and perhaps a more classic "American College" experience. Such schools often have bigger perks for athletes because the schools stands to gain financially when it's athletes succeed.

When considering various size or types of schools there's a few important things to keep in mind. While bigger schools certainly provide a unique social environment, a bigger school also means you can get lost in the crowd.

Schools with 20, 30 or even 50 thousands students often create very different academic environments, classrooms with hundreds if not thousands of students in a given lecture, etc. Smaller institutions and "liberal arts" schools tend to have a greater focus on the undergraduate academic experience, and better student/faculty ratios. *Note:a lot of larger schools do have "Honors Colleges," sections of the school where you can be surrounded by other academically rigorous people and professors etc. Just because you want to go to a big school and have a stereotypical American college experience doesn't necessarily mean that you have to completely forego serious academics.

3-Costs

Costs are obviously an enormous component when it comes to selecting a school. Varying costs are one of the most important reasons to pursue various schools where you might end up at.

Sometimes for some reason a coach just won't have a lot of scholarship money to give out on a given year. It may not be a reflection on your ability or even the coaches interest in you. But a lot of things need to align to create a positive college athlete experience. By pursuing lots of different options, you can insure that you aren't going to fall through the cracks, or get caught paying way more than you should when a coach offers you less scholarship than you might deserve.

The out of pocket costs of college vary drastically. For the first time this year the full costs of the most expensive schools reached $70,000. At the same time, every year new financial aid and scholarships become available. My general counsel is that as an athlete, unless there is a very compelling reason, you should never be paying full-price to go to school. If the school or the coach is not able to help you find funding of some

8

sort, than they aren't particularly invested in having you there, and it's probably not a good fit. In chapters 3 and 4, we go into detail about how to navigate discussions about scholarships with coaches, academic scholarships, and financial aid.

While the exact costs of a given school may not become clear till late in the game, there are a few ways filtering by costs can be useful. Coaches at public "State-Schools" can sometimes offer you "in State" tuition". Private universities often have a much higher initial cost, but at the same time they also may offer extensive "need based" aid. On the U.S News website you can filter by, "best financial" aid, etc.

4-Level of the team

Joining a team that is the right level for you is critical for your development as a player and your experience as a student. You can be at your dream school, but if you aren't a good fit on the level of the team, it can to seriously affect your experience.

It can be very enticing if a coach at a lower level school may offer you a large scholarship, and expect you to play high in the line-up your first year. If the costs are a central priority for you, you may commit to the school that offers you the most scholarship. From a tennis perspective, however, it may not be the best thing to play right at the top of the line-up as a freshmen. It leaves no room for improvement, and if you are the best player on your team, then you are probably helping the other players rise to your level rather than being challenged to improve yourself.

At the same time, it can be very difficult for a junior player who has had a lot of success to come into a team and not-even make the line up. As much as you may not want to play #1 your freshman year, it is probably worse to be stuck forever at 7, 8, 9 on the team is never fun. The majority of players who don't start there freshmen year, never end up starting. Cause for every good player that graduates and opens up a spot in the line-up, the coach is also trying to recruit to fill that spot with a new good player.

As your take stock of your level and that of a given college, it is probably best to try and aim for a school where you can make an immediate contribution to the team, where the coach is excited to have you, but where you will still be challenged and have room to improve and move up.

When Luke was considering going to Westmont, he realized that the tennis level was so low that although the was offered a full-scholarship, he was probably not going to improve significantly or enjoy tennis as much for its own sake. He was effectively making tennis "my job,". It would be a means of paying for my college experience, rather than the fun and rewarding part of that college experience that it can me. At the same time, I was also offered a small scholarship at Baylor University, who was #3 in the country at the time. While I was drawn to the possibility of playing for a "big-time" program and even competing for a national title, after going and seeing a match at

9

Baylor I realized that the level was probably a little bit too high for me. I could have scraped and clawed to play #3 doubles or maybe a little singles, but I was never going to be a big-time contributor, and in all likelihood I was going to effectively be converted into a practice partner for the "real" players. It's often best to consider schools where you will be challenged, but not thoroughly discouraged. Where both the players and the coach feel they are lucky to have made "the match". In the chapter "Analyzing my Level" we'll go into greater detail on how to establish your level and thus what level schools you should be considering.

5-Coaching dynamic

While it's generally not advisable to choose a school just for the coach, your college coach is going to have a big impact on your experience at the school and in the tennis program. A good relationship can make your time there, while struggling in this area can ruin an entire college experience or make you want to transfer schools.

It is important to keep in mind that there is a fair amount of job changing among coaches. This is especially true of assistant coaches, who will constantly move on after even just a year or two. During your discussions with coaches, it's totally fair game to ask the coach how long he is planning on staying at the institution. Keep in mind that it is probably in the coaches interest to make you think he is going to stay indefinitely. Ultimately the coach can be a factor in what school you choose, but you also have to consider what your time at the school/program will be like in the case that the coaches does move on.

6-Location

This one doesn't need a lot of explaining. Do you want to go to school right in the heart of a big city, or will you prefer a rural campus? Some universities are right by the coast, or near a particularly city where you might want to work after graduation.

The only thing worth noting here which a lot of students (especially international students) miss, is that winter happens! While you are on campus before you commit to the school--and I can't recommend more highly making sure to get on campus and get a feel for the team and the coach and the facilities--make sure to ask how much the team plays indoors versus outdoors. Also make sure that you see both the indoor and the outdoor facilities.

7-Religious affiliation

Most colleges no longer have official religious affiliation, but those that do sometimes have certain requirements for students: weekly chapel attendance, a religious studies

10

course, etc. The requirements don't tend to be to demand-
ing, but they are worth knowing about beforehand.
On the other hand, if you are looking for a school with a specific religious affiliation, that
is a great way to narrow down your search from the start. Coaches at such schools are
often eager to recruit players who actually want that religious element in their
education--often because the coaches are tired of having to sell that element to athletes
who view that aspect as downside.

Know the important factors for you!

When it came time for Luke's sister Ellie to begin her college search, she knew that she wanted to go to school in California. She was also pretty sure that she wanted to go to a Christian school. Knowing even just these two factors helped narrow her search down to just a few dozen school, rather than the thousands that she could have applied to with her stellar grades. After nar-rowing her search, Ellie was able to take into consideration how much the coaches were interested in her, what kind of academic/athletic scholarships each school could offer her, and also those intangibles that make a good school the right "fit"--somewhere where she intuitively knew she might thrive.

In this case Ellie she was able to narrow down the schools she was interested by geography, religious affiliation, and tennis level. But many athletes don't have such clear preferences. By considering the important factors for you, you can simplify your process and end up at a school that is a good fit for you!

There's a whole world of websites and tools to help you begin this search. It can often be overwhelming. It often isn't so easy to narrow the search. One great way to discover specific univer-sities that might be a good fit, is to look at universities playing schedules. If there's one university you are interested, look on the school's athletic website and find out what conference they are in. By looking at any team's schedule you'll be able to see what schools they play against. Often schools are in the same "conference"[1] as other schools with similar qualities.

If you contact one coach but he doesn't have space for you or doesn't show interest, other schools in the same "conference" might display similar characteristics.

---

[1] Athletic programs in all divisions are divided into different "athletic conferences". While teams often plays against other schools not in their conference, the conferences composes the teams which a given school plays against every year. The winners of each conference often represent the conference at the national level at the end of the year, playing against the other conference winners.

11

Remember, just because one school isn't interested in you, doesn't mean a similar school won't be. Luke and *Anonymous* each had extensive email or phone communication with no less than 15 schools during just my senior year of high school!

Tools for university research

https://nces.ed.gov/collegenavigator/Is a massive database with a bunch of statistics on every school in the U.S! Don't believe everything a coach tells you! Do your own research! https://www.ncaa.org/Is the governing body of all NCAA (Division 1, 2 , and 3). All the official rules and schedules are published on this website. When it comes time to getting NCAA clearance or permission to play, you will have to go through this site. https://www.usnews.com/best-collegesBreaks down each college into many categories and ranks them all. This is a helpful tool if you want to know the difference betwee colleges academically.

12

CHAPTER 3: MAKING THE CONNECTION

If you are a top player, maybe a lot of school are reaching out to you. But you can't depend on the perfect school to just find you randomly. No matter how good of a player you are, if you don't have the right exposure, you are never going to be discovered by the right coach, nor will you have the credibility for them to want to take a risk on you with a spot on the team or or a scholarship. While coaches are constantly looking for players, you have to take your interest into your own hands.

The Power of Connections

The world of tennis is very small. Everyone tends to know everyone. The world gets even smaller when it comes to coaches. In college tennis the coaches are always communicating with each other, talking about the upcoming recruiting class.

Think of getting to the right school for you as your first forays into adult networking. Reach out to players or coaches already within the schools that you may be considering.

Luke was not on the radar screen of the Princeton coach until very late in the recruiting season (we cover the timeline of recruiting in chapter 4). Luke had been communicating with the Wake Forest coach. When it became clear that Luke wasn't going to go to Wake Forest, the Wake Forest coach mentioned Luke's name to the Princeton coach. These stories are everywhere. Coaches often find their players through other coaches.

What this means for the players is that they have to be a class act *all*the time, not just when a specific coach is watching. The information coaches share with each other involves the level of a player, but also their character (how they behave themselves on court), and other thoughts, like if they could handle being part of a strong academic program, etc.

Reputation as a player can make or break your college process! Usually, if a player carries a negative reputation it is enough for coaches to turn the other way. It is important to ensure that as a player you carry yourself as you wished to be perceived. If you are unsure about what connotations lie behind your name ask people you really trust to go and find out. Don't ask the people you train with, this will not be an honest answer. No one wants confrontation.

13

I have known players whose reputation alone have earned them a spot into a top University – especially international players known for being a good tennis player, but also for having great sportsmanship, and a great work-ethic.This is most valuable when coaches are struggling to find their last player for their recruiting class. Coaches can get a little desperate and rush their decision, and if they only hear good things about a specific player they won't hesitate in offering up a spot in their line-up.

It is very hard for coaches to be up to date on every player, so they often to rely on the information given by the people they trust. If I am asked my opinion about a particular player. I usually have to describe their reputation as a person, their style of play and if I see any potential in them. Ultimately, what a coach wants to know is: *will this player be a good fit for my team?* It is important to start asking yourself this question of yourself, and to change anything that may be a negative factor for coaches

How to talk to a College Coach

Coaches go through countless interviews with potential recruits every year. This can be in the form of a video call or through email and messages.

The first time you speak with a college coach via a video call it is a perfect opportunity to show how good of a recruit you are. Coaches love to hear enthusiasm for tennis. Specially mentioning an interest in carrying on a carrier in tennis (going pro) after college. This shows that you will take your time in college seriously and will be committed to always improving. They also like to hear about any non-tennis interests you may have. This is because some schools don't just want to accept single minded students (especially if the school is very academic). A university wants to attract interesting people who tend to pursue multiple passions. Therefore, since a coach is in contact with admissions, while you are in conversation with the coach he will be simultaneously thinking how I can sell this student to admissions - is he interesting, does he bring more to the table than just tennis.

Since coaches tend to do a lot of interviews with recruits online. It is important to make a good impression and not to bore them when having a Skype call. The typical type of questions that coaches get during an interview are:

- What is a typical day like for a player?
- How much tennis do you play as a team?
- How many individual sessions can I have?
- What are the facilities like?

14

Sports USA has a great list of generic questions you can ask a coach, https://www.unitedsportsusa.com/blog/questions-college-coaches-recruiting.

While these are important questions for you to understand what your experience at the school will be like, it is important to also have other questions to ask the coach. One very effective way of grasping the coaches attention is, when the time is right, thinking of new questions that may catch them off guard. A quick tip is to write down a list of questions on a piece of paper that you can keep besides your computer while you are communicating with them. This way if you feel you get stuck or get a bit nervous and forget the next question, you can just glance down quickly and ask away.

You could even turn the interview around by imposing the thinking and questions to him.

Such as:

- What makes your University better than [insert competitor school]
- I have an interest in [insert legitimate interest be honest], will I be able to do this at your Universites.
- What type of atmosphere are you trying to create at your tennis program? What type of people are you trying to recruit. Usually this type of question will reveal a lot about a university. It is important to know you will fit in with the existing team.

Before talking to the coach it is worth looking at the team's roster, results, photos of the facilities etc. If they have had a good result recently, mention this during your conversation. "I noticed you had a very good win (or close match) against…. Could you tell me what the team is usually like/ what the atmosphere/ how exciting the match was?" Straight away you will have the coaches attention. It shows you are interested and engaged, and their interested in you as a recruit will grow immediately. All you had to do was google their program's name and look at results.

Online Communication Guidelines

It is not always easy to show your real self through the internet. Every email interaction and text message counts. You will do your best by following a few simple things:

- Avoid short answers. If you want to be engaging with coaches, simple one word answers will not do. It is your job to sell yourself.
- Always Spell check. This is specially true if you come from a non-english speaking country. You are trying to show the coach you are academically prepared, and constant spelling errors may send the incorrect message.
- Relax a little, if a coach has already reached out. It means they are already interested. You have the upper hand.

15

The big No No's:

No white lies about grades to coaches. If a coach is serious. They are in communication with admissions. Any wrong miscommunication can result in denied entry to a school.

During your communication with coaches it is best to be transparent about your tennis results. There is no easy way to tell a coach about bad result. Coaches tend to check plenty of results. If a match result of yours has been posted on the UTR system, you can expect the coach who you are talking to to have already seen it. While there is no reason to draw attention to a rough patch of matches, losses can provide an opportunity to show the coach your mental and emotional maturity. You can highlight some positive things you take away from a loss, or how you plan to better prepare for your following match. This can build a relationship of trust from the very beginning, which is very important once you are part of their team.

Facebook Guidelines

Facebook is perhaps your most powerful tool to communicate with coaches. Every college coach has an account which they use to reach out to college players. If they see a good result from an international tournament, they will type in that name into facebook and send a quick message.

It is of huge importance to keep your social media presentable! Most players are personable enough in face to face interactions, but one common pitfall which a lot of internationals aren't always prepared for is keeping up a presentable social media presence. Particularly when you take into consideration that coaches may even be first reaching out to you via social media, your profiles serve as your first impression, so it it can be very important to keep social media presentable. Furthemore, while coaches may not always be concerned, the admissions departments of university will actively look over an applicant's social media for any redflags. One policy that is worth adopting is to remove from your profile any and all photos that have alcohol or any substances--even if you aren't consuming them, or even if they are legal in your country. Remember in the United States the legal drinking age is 21, so even if you are of legal drinking age in your own country, a photo of you with alcohol can unfortunately be a cause for trouble.

Go back through the oldest of photos, and any comments that may be found in those photos to see if there is anything inappropriate that needs to be removed. Furthermore, do not be in groups or associated with pages that can be considered inappropriate, racist, or obscene. In 2017, Harvard rescinded the admission offers of 10 students who posted inappropriate memes on what they thought was a private page.

16

Missed Messages from Coaches

If a person on facebook has no friends in common with you, a message from them might go into "filtered messages". During recruiting be sure to check these messages on Facebook. A college coach might not want to add you as a friend, but they may send you a message. Luke only learned this after arriving at Princeton. He discovered that two other Ivy league coaches had sent him messages and he had completely missed them. This book isn't Facebook 101 but we just don't want someone else to miss out on a good opportunity because they didn't know.

You can find these "Filtered" messages only through the desktop version of Facebook. You then select the messenger app. Once within this page, if you click options: a four additional options will appear; Active contacts, Message Requests, Archive Threads, Unread Threads. It is advisable to go through all of them just to be safe. Within Message requests tab there will be an additional link to open the **filtered messages** tab. More often than not. Specially if you have being doing well in tournaments (particularly international tournaments) you will find a message or two from college coaches showing some interest in you. When I first looked at my filtered messages I was surprised at the amount of messages I had no idea existed. Apologies to all the foreign players who asked me to play doubles.

17

CHAPTER 4: EVENT TIMELINE

The exact time when you can start talking to coaches has moved earlier and earlier over the last several years. As a general rule, the NCAA prohibits college coaches from contacting high school students before September 1st of the athlete's Junior year (grade 11). However, this doesn't mean *you* can't reach out to coaches before then! There are no rules against you initiating contact. This means you need to be proactive! If there is a school that you want to go to, or even a coach that you want to talk to, reach out to them. You have to make it happen. Send an introductory email with a head-shot, your tennis resume (best wins, rankings, upcoming schedule) and express interest in the program. Do your homework on how the team has done recently. When they have a big win, it might be a good time to send the coach an email, congratulating the team and expressing your interest in the program.

Check the NCAA Recruitment Calendar to learn about the rules regarding when coaches can contact you.

Ideally, you should start the scholarship recruiting process as early as possible. The earlier you start, the more time you will have to make any changes which will affect your eligibility (such as improving your grades) and negotiating scholarships with coaches.

If you are starting later than the start of your junior year, you can still use these steps to get an athletic scholarship – but your process will be more accelerated.

Freshman year (Grade 9)

- Research NCAA and NAIA Eligibility Requirements: make sure you are taking the right high school courses for eligi-

bility.
- Work on improving your tennis and develop a plan to play the right tournaments to let your tennis be discovered.
- If possible, attend a few college matches so you can begin to get a sense of the level needed to be a part of the team.

Sophomore Year (Grade 10)
- Check Eligibility: Make sure you are on track with your grades and courses so you are eligible for the NCAA and NAIA
- Develop Leadership Skills: Now is a good time to volunteer as a counsellor at a camp, give sports lessons, or prove your leadership abilities in other ways, such as non-athletic extracurricular activities.
- Make an initial one page athlete "CV" or "Resume" highlighting who you are, your GPA, your best athletic results.

18

- Make an initial recruiting video; at least begin to record some of your matches.
- Research Colleges: Make a list of colleges you would like to attend and write down the coach contact info.
- Send Coaches Info: Write letters of introduction to coaches and send them your resume.

Junior Year

- Update resume/CV: Update your portfolio with the latest information and video
- Contact Coaches: There are now periods when coaches are allowed to reach out to you. Contact them to show your interest. They may give you a call back!
- Plan College Visits: You can make "unofficial" visits to colleges and meet coaches. Many athletes verbally commit to an agreement with a coach during their junior year.
- Make aList of Questions for Coaches: See chapter 3 "Making the Connection" for a list of ideas.
- Prepare for and take the SAT/ACT and/or TOEFL tests - depending on the school's requirements.

Senior Year

- Learn Contact Rules: Coaches are only allowed to contact you during certain periods. Learn these periods so you can maximize contact opportunities.
- Here's the link to the NCAA guide for recruiting rules for all Divisions. http://www.ncaa.org/student-athletes/resources/recruiting-calendars
- Retake SAT: Retake the standardized tests if you aren't satisfied with your scores
- Practice Talking to Coaches: You can now go to official visits with coaches and meet with them off campus, so practice speaking to them and representing yourself.
- Evaluate Scholarship Offers: Make a list of scholarship offers you receive and determine what is really included

- Negotiate Offers: Early on, you will have more leeway to negotiate for a better scholarship.
- Do not assume it all happens straight away. Coaches will be talking to multiple players at once. Therefore, they may take their time before offering a spot on the line-up to you.
- Make a Decision: Make sure you are satisfied with the offer. Once you've decided, it is time to sign theLetter of Intent.

19

Because of how much of the recruiting happens through word of mouth and different coaches hearing about players from other coaches, it is often better to get into the recruiting communication game earlier. Luke was mainly considering Division III and NAIA schools during his sophomore year. It wasn't until the start of his junior year that he had a few breakthrough wins, and began advancing further in ITFs, that the possibility of playing on a high level Division I team became a possibility.

"Junior" year, or grade 11, is when most of the process happens.

The recruiting process culminates in an agreement between a coach and a player. College coaches can give verbal promises to student athletes, but are not necessarily binding. What really matters is signing the National Letter of Intent (NLI). This is a formal agreement between the prospective student and the institution which states: A prospective student-athlete agrees to attend the institution full-time for one academic year; the institution formalizes the financial agreement for one academic year once you sign a National Letter of Intent with a college, you have committed yourself to that school. You cannot withdraw from the NLI and sign with another school. There is an early signing date (usually in November of the senior year), and a regular signing period in April of senior year. Check out theNational Letter of Intent websiteto learn more.

What to Expect on Official Visits

Official visits usually represent the last stride of a player's recruiting process. You are allowed to take up to 5 official visits during your senior year. The coach invites you to spend two whole days at the university where you will meet the team, see the campus and facilities, get to experience classes and basically see all the university has to offer. During an "unofficial" visit, a coach is not allowed to pay for your travel, accommodations, or meals. But an official visit is fully funded by the university.

Official visits are not always offered to players. If a school wants to bring you on campus for an official visit, it is a very good sign that they are interested in you and are considering offering you at least some sort of scholarship. A lot of players end up making a decision before their senior year, so never really have the chance to take an official visit. However, an official visit is the perfect opportunity to see whether a university is a match made in heaven, and can be central for your final decision process.

20

Anonymous: "I personally decided to visit four Universities. I had spent a lot of time talking to multiple coaches from universities from all over the country. However, after making my table of pros and cons and considering every possible option – comparing academics, tennis and what I thought of the coaches – I was able to narrow my choices down to four. Once I had my top four universities I notified the coaches that I wouldn't be able to make a final decision without having seen the universities in person. One of the coaches wasn't particularly happy since he was pressuring me to make a decision as soon as possible. "

A coach may often pressure you into a decision. They do this so that they get you early enough before any other coach makes you an offer. You want to avoid being rushed into a decision, unless you truly know what the right thing to do.

If you live a long way away from the universities you are considering, you can organize with the coaches so that you don't have to fly back home between visiting each school. Coaches can talk to each other to coordinate dates and flights so that they can spread the cost of the trip and to make the visits more time effective.

Anonymous didn't quite know what to expect once he left London for his four official visits. But it doesn't take very long to realize what an official visit is all about. In simple terms, you become the VIP. You are treated incredibly well. Coaches will try their best to impress you, so enjoy it.
"I was even taken to one of the best steakhouses in America. I was not complaining." -*Anonymous*

Coaches tend to schedule your visit so that you make the most of your time. Therefore, you don't really get many chances to rest. You are taken from place to place, meeting one person after another - including faculty members. Essentially you get to meet and see anything that may be important to you. They definitely do their best to impress you with everything the university has to offer.

The type of university you visit will have a lot to do with the style of visit you may have. If you visit a big college school, you can even expect to be taken to a party or two by the players.

Anonymous had a strong interest in engineering, so a big part of his visit was meeting the professors in the field. At the same time, he wanted to get to know the people he would share four years of his life. An official visit is a great opportunity to get a better sense of the team dynamics, an aspect which can be a defining factor for an athlete.

21

Remember that although during an official visit the coaches and the players of the team are most likely trying to convince you to come to their school, until you sign a National Letter of Intent and officially commit, you are also being observed and considered. If you behave inappropriately during the visit, it can jeopardize your chances of getting admitted.

Anonymous summarized his recruiting season in words that are true for a lot of people that go through this process, "Each visit was draining. I had to make sure I was always engaged with the conversations I had, which was not easy whilst battling jet lag.

However, I would not have been able to pick the right university had I not visited then. It is very easy to be influenced by rankings and people's opinions; however, ultimately nothing is more powerful and true than the feeling you have whilst on a visit."-- *Anonymous* says.

22

CHAPTER 5:
STANDARDIZED TESTS

For athletes, it is a requirement for all NCAA programs, most NAIA programs, and most Junior-Colleges. International students for whom English is not their primary language, will have to take the Test of English as a Foreign Language (TOEFL), and all students will have to take either the Standardized Aptitude Test (SAT) or the American College Testing Program (ACT).

Take these tests as soon as possible! There are only benefits for taking these tests sooner than later.

-You can set it up so the tests aren't immediately reported to universities.

- You can only benefit from the practice of taking it earlier. You find out relatively where you stand.

- You can practice and retake the SAT, ACT and TOEFL as many times as you want.

-Taking the tests more than once corresponds with getting higher average scores. - Of course, they are not free, so bear the cost in mind

-A lot of schools will "super-score" which means they combine your best English score, with your best math score, even if they were taken at different times. This further incentivises taking the tests numerous times. Maybe one day you are "off" in English but you crush the math, or vice versa.

- Find out where and when you can take the tests as they may be limited in your area. Also, it is good to consider the time it takes for results to come out. You wouldn't want to miss an application deadline.

Athletes *only* get into trouble or get caught in tight situations when they haven't taken any of these tests soon enough. You don't want to be in a situation where a coach says, "I need you to get X score," and you only have one chance to get the score in time. Take the test early and relieve that stressful situation!

We recommend taking the SAT or ACT between October and February of your 11th grade year. This is not meant to be discouraging for juniors or seniors or even graduates who haven't started the process yet. In **Eligibility and Amateurism**, we discuss how to jump-start your process if you are late at starting the process, and some strategies for preserving your eligibility to play a full four years of college tennis. But for those who have time to prepare, mid-way through your junior year will give you an

23

accurate measure of where you are, but will also allow you a significant window to make progress.

Test Tutoring and Practice books

There are tons of online and local services that provide tutoring for the SAT, TOEFL, and ACT. While these can be pretty expensive, investing in a few lessons will provide effective test-taking methods that can boost your score quickly. The long-term investment is most likely worth it.

Remember, most colleges can combine athletic and academic scholarships. A couple hundreds points on your SAT score can mean thousands of dollars of scholarship every year. Furthermore, high grades and good SAT/ACT scores will make you more attractive to university coaches.

Even if you don't want to invest in SAT/ACT tutoring, there is a huge number of resources you can take advantage of to prepare and practice. https://blog.prepscholar.com/best-sat-prep-books_https://blog.prepscholar.com/best-act-prep-books

This is a great website explaining the differences between various SAT and ACT prep books. Most books come with numerous practice tests so you can practice and get used to the pace of these test, check your answers slowly, see where you went wrong, etc. There are also remote tutors. If you are a player who is travelling for international tournaments, it is easy to schedule a session with a tutor remotely, where you can work together through Skype™/ Facetime™ and they can leave you homework remotely.

ACT versus SAT

There is plenty of information online about the differences between the SAT and the ACT. Which one is right for you? Luke took the SAT while *Anonymous* took the ACT. The SAT is out of a score of 1600 points, 800 for the math and 800 for the English section. There is also an optional writing section which is now a score out of 10.

The ACT is scored out of 36. Your score on the English, Math,

Reading and Science sections is all out of 36, and then averaged. So, for example, let's say you received a

25 on English, 32 on Math, 28 on Reading, and 24 on Science. Your overall composite score would be (25+32+28+25)/4 = 27.5, rounded to the nearest whole number, it would be 28. (It's icing on the cake when you get to benefit from the rounding up!

Which test should you take? That's a question we are going to outsource to people who think the differences are a lot greater and more important than we do! A quick google of

24

"differences between ACT and SAT" will initiate you into a long and heated debate

about which one you should take.

https://www.studyusa.com/en/a/1305/act-vs-sat-ultimate-guide-to-choosing-the-right-tes

tis a great summary website that can help lead you in the right direction.

Test Links

Test of English as a Foreign Language (TOEFL)

https://www.ets.org/toefl/ibt/register/centers_dates

Standardized Aptitude Test (SAT)

https://collegereadiness.collegeboard.org/sat/register

American College Testing Program (ACT) http://www.act.org/content/act/en/products-and-services/the-act/registration.html

25

CHAPTER 6: RANKINGS AND RATINGS AND VIDEOS

Athletes are always asking questions such as, "What ranking do I need to achieve to be recruited by this school?" or "If I get ranked in the top 25 will I get a full scholarship?" or "What combination of SAT, grades and ranking must I have to play in the Ivy league?"

There is no definitive number in response to these questions and whoever gives you one, may be wrong. There is no clear mathematical formula for athletic college scholarships. It is at best a complex and vague combination of many factors. There is, in this sense, no way to "hack" the system. Ultimately, you have to just be what coaches want. What's great is that most coaches desire a lot of the same things. Still, it's helpful to know what metrics college coaches are using, what they look out, and what sort of numbers they will find compelling.

In the United States, the most popular metric that coaches use is still https://tennisrecruiting.net/. If you are mainly playing in the United States, you are already within this system. The system automatically keeps track of your matches in all sanctioned events.

It has become increasingly popular in recent years for international players to try and play tournaments in the United States in order to gain "exposure". In general, there are significantly simpler, cheaper, and more effective ways for international athletes to gain credibility than to try and establish residence in a U.S state, get registered with the tennisrecruiting.netand a establish a 1-5 star ranking by playing U.S tournaments.

Furthermore, as popular as tennisrecruiting.com is among college coaches, the Universal Tennis Rating system,https://myutr.com/is becoming increasingly popular. The Universal Tennis Rating system, or "UTR" as it is known, places all players on a 16 points scale. The top pros are all above 15.5. The very best college players are in the range of 14. Coaches will often have unstated thresholds, "this year we are looking for 13.3's or higher", etc.

A leading proponent of UTR, Dave Fish, head men's tennis coach at Harvard University, states that "The Universal Tennis Rating system is now being recognized by many college coaches as the best metric available for judging junior talent." Currently, more than 40 national tennis federations submit all of their tournament results to UTR.

26

LUKE GAMBLE

The matches in most tournaments will be reported to the UTR. You can search for UTR specific events athttps://myutr.com/ events. In the UK for example, they have begun to implement a few exclusive UTR tournaments every year.

If you send an email introducing yourself to a coach, it will be very easy for the coach to look you up and get an accurate sense of your level. It's also very easy to sign up for a personal account athttps://myutr.com/where you can see your rating, and then send that directly to coaches.

Is ranking or results more important?

Ultimately, all that matters is the level you have, and whether you can demonstrate that level. You want to choose a tournament schedule that gives you the opportunity to play against good players, and also establish a good ranking. Picking the right schedule is key. Ultimately there is no hiding your level. Some players pursue inflated rankings by travelling to remote areas for easier points. Coaches might be initially impressed by the ranking. But they tend to be pretty good at analysing the significance of a certain ranking. Ultimately you'll also only end up deceiving yourself.

While it may be attractive to try and inflate your ranking to better increase your chances of scholarship. If you arrive to the university and you aren't nearly at the level that the coach expects, you are going to end up in a very difficult situation where the coach is going to want to cut your scholarship, or may not give you a chance to play as much during matches. Though scholarships are awarded on an annual basis, and it is frowned upon for a coach to lower or cut a player's scholarship because their play did not live up to expectations, there is no rule clearly outlawing the practice. See http://www.ncaa.org/about/frequently-asked-questions-about-ncaafor more information.

When considering your schedule try and balance the following three criteria: tournaments that can help raise your ranking; 2- tournaments that give you a chance to play high level players to show what you can do; 3- Tournaments that can give you exposure and a chance to be discovered by coaches.

Doubles or Singles?

The college matches format is 6 singles matches and three doubles per match. College coaches may not pay as much attention to players who don't have interest in playing doubles. It can be a sign that you aren't really a "team" player. Even if doubles is not your strength, make sure that you are working on your volleys, playing in the tournaments that offer doubles, and can at perform at a decent level on the doubles

27

court. Show the coaches with results that you are capable of playing good doubles. In some cases, a very good doubles ranking may be more impressive to a coach than a normal singles ranking.

Don't fall between the cracks!

But what do you do if you fall between the cracks? What if you are from a small nation that doesn't have many tennis players? Maybe you are four time national champion, but it's hard for a coach to know what that means, and the federation might not be reporting the results on UTR. Maybe you are ranked highly in an area where it doesn't necessarily make sense to the coach.

Remember that you can't depend on coaches to suddenly find you. You can sit on your couch hoping that the love of your life is going to just walk into your living room, but you stand a much better chance if you go out and either take the initiative or at least give yourself the chance to be seen. It may mean spending a little extra money and travelling to a series of junior or professional ITF tournaments in your region. It could also mean finding a coach that will help you get set up to play a month of tournaments on a nearby country, where you can establish a ranking from that system which you can then advertise to coaches. You aren't going to be discovered by accident. Go out and put yourself in the position where good things can happen. If you can't think of anything, email a few coaches introducing yourself, explaining that you are a good player, passionate about the game, and are interested in playing college tennis. They are in the business of finding hidden gems, more than likely they will respond with some advice or even show some initial interest themselves.

Recruiting Videos

Especially when you don't have a robust or recognized tournament schedule or ranking to demonstrate to coaches, it can be helpful to have a recruiting video. A quick YouTube of "tennis-recruiting videos" yields thousands of examples of how you can go about making your own video.

Here are a few 'do's' and 'dont's' when it comes to making your own video:

Do keep the video short.
Do put your name in the title of the video.
Do show your shots from various angles--maybe a minute of every shot, 30 seconds from two different angles. You should aim to keep the hitting part of the video to 10 minute maximum.

28

Do include match play. You can include this after the hitting section, or even upload a separate video. The match play segment should be around 10-20 minutes of point play. In order to get used to playing in front of the camera, you can start having your parent or a friend consistently record various parts of your matches. Within 5 or 10 matches you'll be able to identify a good segment of a match that is representative of your tennis.

Do start the video by introducing yourself and explaining what year you are graduating from high-school, etc.

Don't edit out all of your errors. Some players do so, and pretend to be perfect. College coaches will laugh at such videos. The point is for the coaches to get a sense of your strokes, your physique, and how you hit the ball. They will also be looking at your potential – how much you can improve.

Don't be vague about your graduation dates or year.

A recruiting video is not necessary for all players, and it certainly can't replace match play and results, but it can be a powerful tool to get on the radar screen when you aren't in a country or system where you have a meaningful ranking, etc. For example, Luke was junior national champion of Costa Rica for 3 years in a row...no colleges cared. He decided to go to Guatemala to play an ITF and get a chance to play against some better players. He had his mom video tape every match. After the tournament, he cropped part of the final match and uploaded it to YouTube. In the end Luke's ITF ranking wasn't stellar, but when the Princeton coach, Billy Pate, saw the video of Luke serving and volleying, it immediately captured his interest. In the end, there will be several factors that end up affecting your road to your college choice, but a well done video can definitely help get that process started.

29

CHAPTER 7: ELIGIBILITY AND AMATEURISM

The collegiate model of sports is centered on the fact that those who participate are students first and not professional athletes.

This means that while you can play professional tournaments before going to college, the NCAA rules are meant to insure that the players are "amateurs". They don't want Roger Federer coming back and trying to get a college tennis scholarships. While for most people this is no problem at all, it is important to keep up to date with the NCAA regulations, particularly those surrounding *academic* eligibility.

For NCAA divisions I and II, the NCAA eligibility center carries out a standard amateurism certification through theEligibility Center. The process is a collaborative effort among student-athletes, the colleges and universities they hope to attend and the NCAA Eligibility Center. In Division III, amateur certification is completed solely by the school.

The amateurism certification process begins when student-athletes register with the Eligibility Center. Each prospective student-athlete is asked several questions about his or her sports-participation history. If the answers indicate a possible violation of amateurism standards, the amateurism certification staff works with the college or university to determine the facts. If a violation of amateurism standards occurred, a penalty will be imposed based on the severity of the violations. Penalties include repayment of money, sitting out a specified number of games or, in rare cases, permanent ineligibility. You should sign up with the eligibility center as early as your junior year.

Pro tennis, Prize money and College Eligibility.

It used to be that if a player accepted any prize money, they had to document that the prize money didn't exceed their expenses. The NCAA has got a lot more relaxed on tennis player prize money, partially because it is so hard to make significant prize money. Here are the official rules from the NCAA regarding prize money and eligibility:

"In all sports except tennis, a student-athlete or prospective student-athlete may accept prize money as long as the amount of the prize is less than or equal to his or her

30

expenses for participating in the competition, such as meals or lodging. The prize money may not pay for expenses of parents or coaches.

In tennis, a prospective student-athlete may accept up to $10,000 per year in prize

money. Once he or she has accepted $10,000 in prize money in a particular year, he or

she may accept additional prize money on a per-event basis as long as the amount of

the prize does not exceed his or her expenses. A current tennis student-athlete may

accept prize money as long as the amount of the prize is less than or equal to his or her

expenses for participating in the competition."

Source:http://www.ncaa.org/about/frequently-asked-questions-about-ncaa

Academics and Eligibility

The two most common reasons that players are deemed in-eligible or lose years of college eligibility, is when they take time off during or after high-school.

The length of eligibility for a student-athlete varies by division. A Division I student-athlete has five calendar years to compete in four seasons of competition, while a Division II or III student-athlete has 10 semesters or 15 quarters of full-time enrolment to compete in four seasons of competition.

In most cases, your "five years of eligibility" begins the year that you graduate from high-school. This is particularly important for players that have finished high-school and for some reason or another didn't go directly towards college tennis.
Important: If you play tournaments after graduating from high-school, during the year that would be your first year as a college player, you will most likely lose that year of eligibility.

The rules around "Gap Years" for tennis have gotten increasingly strict. The NCAA does not want players graduating from high-school, playing tournaments and training for a year or two, and then enrolling once their tennis level is a lot better. If you take a "gap" year before starting college, do not play ANY tournaments or official matches.

There are a few exemptions that do exist. Military service is the most common exemption. Another exemption is when you take a year off for a religious "mission," the NCAA will not count it as one of your years of eligibility. Again, the important thing is that you don't play tournaments during these windows. If you play even one local tournament and the NCAA finds out about it, they will consider your "GAP" year a training and competition year.

31

In short, if you plan on playing college tennis, it is generally best to proceed immediately to college tennis after graduating from high school. Any delay can easily result in loss of eligibility.

Eligibility Mistakes to Avoid in High-School

The U.S college athletics system is unique because it allows students to be athletes, and athletes to be students. The NCAA is invested in making sure participants are true "student athletes." TheEligibility Centerwill review your high-school transcript. Athletes often run into trouble when they've shortened their high-school education.

Make sure that for each of your semesters, you are enrolled in a full course load. Even if you accidentally get labelled as a part time student during your senior year, it can make it look like you are trying to hide a gap-year.

Especially if you are going to enrol in an online or at a distance high-school, double check and make sure they are an accredited institution. http://www.ncaa.org/student-athletes/future/nontraditional-courses

JuniorColleges

If for some reason you've jeopardized your eligibility, the NCAA will often work with you to preserve at least "some" of your eligibility. In these cases, time is not your friend. If you are ineligible to play for a Division 1, your best option may be to consider starting out at a junior college and then later transferring to a higher program. The NJCAA has significantly less strict rules around eligibility. Though junior colleges sometimes receive a bad reputation, there are a lot of extremely good players at "JuCo's". A lot of former professionals struggled to earn NCAA eligibility so instead they went and played in the junior college leagues.

For example, Damian Hume, played some professional tennis before college, so the NCAA "made" him play a year of junior-college tennis before transferring to an NCAA division 1 program.

Hume had such a good time at his junior college that he decided to stay another year. He ended up leading his team to an undefeated season and the junior college national championship before transferring to Boise State on a full-scholarship.

32

CHAPTER 8: SPORTS SCHOLARSHIP AGENCIES

There are a lot of companies offer services to help match student-athletes with colleges and scholarships. They serve as middle-men between aspiring student athletes, and college coaches.

These agencies are tremendously popular in some circles, and completely absent in others. This is important because if everybody else is doing it, families often feel compelled to sign up with a recruiter. You may feel like if you don't spend the money on such a service, then you have no chance of finding a good school or securing a scholarship. There are a few things you should consider before spending a big fee for an agent.

Reviews and reputation: It is of huge importance to look up reviews and talk to anyone who has previously gone through an agency about the services they were provide. The last thing you want is someone who doesn't really care about you talking to the coaches who have the ability of changing your life.

Tennis specific: Make sure the agency works in tennis, not just "sports". A lot of the agencies specialize in one sport. Few do just tennis, because it is a relatively small market. An agency new to the sport will be learning the process and making the contacts alongside you. They would be as new to the game as you are. This doesn't mean they are a bad agency; nonetheless, you will be much better off going with an agency that has a well established reputation in tennis.

Relationship: There are numerous large recruiting agencies that take on hundreds of athletes every year, and that also work in other sports. If you are going to let an agency represent you or speak on your behalf, make sure it is the right agency and that you have a real relationship with the person who is going to initiate contact with coaches.

Payment structure: Be very clear about your payment structure. Most of the agencies don't post prices for their services online. Some do case by case pricing, etc. While most agencies work on specific consulting prices, some also work based on the commission of a percentage of the scholarship money you earn. Be aware that if this is the case, the agencies incentive might be to send you wherever you get the biggest scholarship, even if it isn't in your best interest or the best fit for you.

33

For all these warnings, it is worth saying that recruiting agencies *have*helped place a lot of players in colleges, and have helped players navigate the perils of recruiting when they might have never even tried.

Principles of a Successful athlete/agent

Anonymous chose to go through an agent to help him with his recruiting process. He had a great experience with his agency. He chose to go through a sport agent because it felt it was too much to attempt to juggle all his responsibilities while adding all the work that goes into recruiting and a college search, "It was too much for me to go through the recruiting process without help. I had to do my own research, keep going to practice, keep performing in tournaments, still do well in school, communicate with coaches and plan skype interviews after school. All of this whilst not really having an idea of what it was I should be doing." For *Anonymous*, getting a sport agent was the right choice.

Agents can't do all the work for you, but their job is just to make your life easier.

Anonymous contracted a small recruiting agency called, " Stars and Stripes Tennis". "Stars and Stripes" is a small tennis recruiting agency run by Pippa Lane. Pippa limits the number of athletes she will work with at a given time. As a result her service is much more tailored to the client. This ensure that she had the time to help each athlete to the best of her abilities. She can meet in person with her athletes, can respond to messages much quicker, and be more invested in her players.

Make sure you are getting individualized attention and you know who exactly is working on your behalf.

Pippa started out by setting up a face to face meeting. *Anonymous* and Pippa then had a very long meeting where they discussed goals, the things *Anonymous*wanted from a university and how to prepare academically to attain these goals. The meeting served as an opportunity for *Anonymous*to gather as much information about the world of tennis in the US. *Anonymous*said, "I was hearing about all the different types of universities, what being a student athlete meant. Meanwhile, what Pippa was doing was

THE COLLEGE TENNIS RECRUITMENT GUIDE

getting a fairly accurate read on me. Her job is to get me into the best university possible, but of course she has to be realistic. She cannot promise everyone that they will get into a top school."

Use the agency to learn. A lot of people worry about impressing the agency, concerned that if the agent doesn't know how good you are then, they won't try and place you at the best schools. It's about you, not the agent.

34

After Pippa had a better read of what *Anonymous'* expectations were, and what academic and tennis level he had at the time, she prepared his CV to send to coaches. This is a short document outlining achievements, both tennis and academically. Pippa aims to present you to coaches as an opportunity for them. From here on, she takes care of all correspondence with the coaches. Meanwhile, she began to promote *Anonymous*among a few select college coaches.

Develop a tennis and academic and personal "CV" or "Resume"; a one page introduction of who you are, your best qualities, your test scores and tournament results.

Pippa always served as a go to person for any questions *Anonymous*had. It is amazing the speed at which she replies to messages or calls from her athletes. Furthermore, she always made sure he was doing whatever was necessary to stay on track for college tennis: ensured that he had his NCAA Eligibility, that he was taking SAT at the right time, and that he was being honest with coaches about any results. Pippa would even show up to my some of his tournaments for support.

It's not just about the end result, the scholarship, the number, the university you end up at. Use the agency to help guide you through the whole process and make your life easier in the interim.

For *Anonymous*it was a huge help having an agent, "Personally, Pippa is now a very close friend of mine. She herself went to college tennis from England when she was a player, so she has been through everything I went through. I still keep in contact with her and if there is anything I may need help with during my time at college, that is tennis related, I can count on her to provide any necessary advice."

Don't let an agent sell you on an impossible dream.

*Anonymous'*experience with Pippa and "Stars and Stripes" is a pretty ideal story. While, *Anonymous'*recruiting story ended pretty happily at top ten academic university, it is important to acquire a recruiting agency that will be realistic with you. It is all fine to dream, but if you have little or no ranking, low SAT/ACT scores, and little else to differentiate you, you cannot expect an agency to miraculously make you appealing to a top ten division school.

35

We know people who have had great experiences with each of these agencies.
Added Sport(United States, India, China, Middle East).
Aussie Athletes Agency(Australia and Oceania)
Stars and Stripes Tennis(United Kingdom)

36

CHAPTER 9: MANAGING EXPECTATIONS

Is college the best four years of your life?

For *Anonymous*, freshman year at his university wasn't quite the dream he thought it was going to be. There's a myth that college is going to be just an epic moment after another. Finally you've made it, and it's all easy sailing from there. Because of the myth surrounding college, a lot of people not only feel unhappy when confronted with reality, but also feel bad for *not* being as happy as expected.

Returning home to the UK after his freshmen, *Anonymous* found that many of his friends who went into college tennis had faced similar challenges *Anonymous'* experience of his first year is compelling summary of the dream but also the challenges most student-athletes face their first year.

"Personally, college tennis became my goal throughout my time in high school. In my head it was all I could think about, and as a result it was put on a pedestal. I thought of American university as this ultimate thing. But as I soon realized after my first year, as are most things, they are what you make of them. Before arriving for my freshmen year, I thought that my level of tennis would suddenly increase because of the style of training I would receive and that I would be competing at a much higher level. I also hadn't really considered the challenges involved with balancing academics with tennis, given the fact that I have always done well in balancing both during my time in high school. Ultimately, my expectation was that I would be having the time of my life. I had seen college tennis as the end goal--the Promised Land."

"But once I got there I realized that nothing is like in the movies, and nothing would ever match up to the expectations I had in my head. My tennis level began to drop. The competition was much tougher than expected and I began to have a match losing streak. This set off a negative attitude in my game that also ended affecting my academics. Struggling in tennis, I began to dedicate too much time in trying to fix my game. This meant that I could place less attention to my academics. This did not reflect well after taking my finals at the end of first term. I began to doubt if the university I was in was the right place for me. Thoughts would run through my head such as, 'I can't believe I'm playing this badly', etc...."

"This was however not the first time something like this had happened to me. And if you are anything like me, chances are you have gone through similar phases in your game or academics where you begin to question things. Having realized the mind-set I had

37

got myself into, I set out to try and find out what the real problem was. I feel that it is important to mention that this happens to many new players to college tennis, and instead of resolving their own problems, and finding the true reason for their issues – they blame their problems on the externals (coaching staff, academics, and facilities). These are the players that usually end up transferring for the wrong reasons.

The answer, as it turned out, was *me.*I could easily have blamed the school, my coaches, my teammates, or "the new culture". But the truth was that I was the problem. It was my unreasonable expectations that prevented me from adapting to this new world I had entered. I'd adopted an unrealistic mentality. Anything that was far from this perfect picture in my head when I first arrived, I dismissed. Decision by decision, this triggered a downwards spiral that ended up affecting the important areas in my life."

"This realization opened my eyes. I was able to begin to see clearly the opportunities that were in front of me. After making this switch in my head, I started to appreciate all I had. I was then able to find a balance, between how much time I can dedicate to my tennis without neglecting my academics. This also led to enjoying all the other aspects that my university had to offer. I can say with certainty that during my first year, I have already made friends for life; memories that I will never forget; and experiences that otherwise, would not have thought possible.

You can't expect the university to do things for you (change your life). Your college years are always what *you*make of them. The university makes you, but you also make the university. Keep working as hard as you always do ensuring you make the most of all the opportunities college tennis has to offer.

"Ultimately, I realized that I was not alone during this process. It took one conversation with friends to realize that most students, if not all, had the same doubts, and were facing similar problems when they first arrived into college. I believe that is what makes the college tennis experience so worth it, is finding a group of friends who have been through similar experiences and are willing to push each other for the greater good of the team. As Teddy

Roosevelt said, 'Nothing in the world is worth having or worth doing unless it means effort, pain, difficulty... I have never in my life envied a human being who led an easy life. I have envied a great many people who led difficult lives and led them well'".

38

APPENDIX: FREQUENTLY ASKED QUESTIONS

What should I do if I just graduated high school and I want to go to the states for college but I haven't done anything yet?

It is best to get started as soon as possible. If it is already the summer after your high-school graduation, it will be difficult to secure a spot at an NCAA school for the fall

– but not impossible. However, by starting communication with coaches, you could start in the spring semester.

After getting contact with coaches, go through the same process outlined in this book, but as fast as possible. Take the SAT/ACT and TOEFL (if abroad). Lastly, given your short time frame, it probably would be a good idea to reach out to some junior colleges. You can always go to a Junior college for at least one year, and if you want you can use your good results and grades to then transfer to an NCAA school for your following year. The most important thing is to just immediately get the ball rolling. Go on the websites of 10 junior colleges and send emails introducing yourself to coaches.

How do I get in touch with college coaches?

All college tennis programs have a website. Google the name of the school and "tennis". Coaches will commonly have their emails or even phone numbers on these websites. If not, they will have a form you can fill out with your information, which will be sent to the coach's email anyways.

Can I take a gap year after high-school and still be eligible to play four years of college tennis?

If you play any tournaments, you will most likely lose a year of eligibility. If you haven't secured a scholarship or at least a spot on the tennis team, a GAP year will often discourage coaches from giving you a spot. If you have already committed to a school and a coach, then you should check with your coach.

What if I get injured and lose my scholarship?

Coaches have the right to lower your scholarship if you become chronically injured or if your level drops significantly. It's not super common, but it does happen. Each scholarship is only an agreement for one year. However, if a coach does lower your scholarship, you will have the opportunity to transfer to a different school. The reason that NCAA allows for "five years to compete in four seasons" is partially to provide for if you get injured and cannot play for a prolonged period of time. Just this last year, for example, Henrik Wiersholm, took a year off because of an injury. He helped the University of Virginia (UVA) win the national title in May of 2017. He did not play during

39

the fall of 2017 or the spring of 2018, but in the fall of 2018 and the spring of 2019 he will again compete for UVA. He will be able to compete for a total of four seasons. So even though he was injured for almost a full year, he will still be able to compete for 4 full years.

However, if you get injured for a couple of months during season you cannot suddenly lose your scholarship. Players are protected by the NCAA, which means scholarships cannot be suddenly removed during an academic year.

40

Made in the USA
Middletown, DE
27 January 2023

23224673R00045